Blacksmithing Beginners

An Easy Guide To Getting Started

Will Kalif

Copyright © 2019 Will Kalif

All rights reserved.

ISBN 13: 978-1-6937-0423-9

Table of Contents

Part I – What you need to get started

A Forge
First Option: Buying a Forge 2
Second Option: Making a Forge 3
Explanation with diagrams of a Forge 4
Different Ways to Make a forge 6
Fuel for your forge 11
Option for you to use rather than coal 12
Tuyere and Blower for your forge 12
Okay, let's talk about anvils 13
Other tools and materials 15

Part II – Doing some Forging

What steel should you start with? 17
Lighting the forge 17
Let's start by ruining a piece of steel 19
The Changing temperature of steel 20
The Heat Properties of steel 22
Let's practice some hammer blows 23
Localized heating and cooling 24
Pointing Steel 25
Angle Hammering 25
Curving steel 27
Cutting steel 29
Let's take a look at an anvil 31
The effects and importance of heat 34
Hardening and tempering steel 36
Annealing 38
Where to get steel 39
One Final Suggestion 40
Resources, Links, and More 42

The Goal of this Book

The goal of this book is to get you started in doing some blacksmithing even though you currently have nothing. You have no forge, no anvil, and no tools. I will give you an exact game-plan for how to get going cheaply and quickly; what you need to get and how to get it.

This isn't a big book on the art of blacksmithing. This is a fast and easy guide to get you started with a basic understanding of what it is, how to do it, and what you need. Whether you want to be a working blacksmith or just pursue it as a hobby doesn't matter. I lay out in this book a good plan for how to get started and I will help you overcome any doubts.

In this book I will tell you exactly what to get and how to get it; or how to make it. This includes a forge and even fuel for your forge.

Thanks for buying my book. Along with it you get email support from me. Please feel free to send me an email if you have blacksmithing questions! *My email is: willkalif@comcast.net*

Note: I have a support web page for all these materials. It includes links and more information about all these supplies and tools:

www.stormthecastle.com/blacksmithing/blacksmithing-ebook-support-page.htm

And if you like videos: I currently have a youtube

playlist with 61 blacksmithing videos that cover many aspects of the craft. Those videos are all available for you to watch on this books support page.

Introduction

Ten years ago I posted my first blacksmithing video to youtube. Back then it was a rather specialized thing and blacksmithing wasn't in the public eye. It was considered an old art that almost nobody practiced anymore.

And that is true. Ten years ago there wasn't a whole lot of interest in the art and craft of blacksmithing. The industrial revolution almost killed it. Factories could now do all the work of a blacksmith at a much faster pace and a much lower cost. The skills that blacksmiths developed over centuries were no longer needed – and almost lost.

But this whole situation turned around in the past decade. Video games, Renaissance faires, youtube, and the internet have all given rebirth to the beautiful art and craft of hammering steel into shape.

Ten years ago you couldn't give away an anvil. Nobody wanted them. Today they are very much sought after and often command a premium price. And this is all quite wonderful.

And this renewed interest in blacksmithing has taken a new shape. The demand isn't so much for the shoeing of horses and the repair of farming tools. Blacksmithing now has taken on an amazingly creative form. It has moved from a functional craft to a very creative and artistic craft.

Every working blacksmith is inundated with requests for hand-made objects like knives, swords, bottle openers, hand-made axes and adzes and so much more. And this is on top of the renewed growth of wrought iron work for fencing, gating, doors and more.

Part of this new allure is the rejection and rebellion against factory made items. There simply is a great pride and admiration for steel and iron objects that have been hand made in the forge. And for good reason – They are beautiful. And they are the result of a combination of skills that are pragmatic in the approach to heating and working metals and artistic in their approach to what the end result will look like.

Times are good for blacksmithing. It's great to see.

Over these years, because of my website and youtube channel I have seen many people start out with the hobby of blacksmithing. And I have fielded many hundreds of questions from people who didn't know how to start.

And this is what this book is all about – helping you to get started in an inexpensive and easy ways. After all you really don't need much to get going in this art.

Safety First – Do not skip this part

When blacksmithing you are dealing with fire, and with metals hot enough to send you directly to the emergency room. It's a serious thing. The fire is not the same temperature as a campfire. It is significantly hotter and significantly more dangerous. So, exercise caution.

Here are some guidelines:

- Wear safety equipment and cotton clothes. This includes wearing long pants. Do not forge while wearing shorts. I also recommend long sleeve shirts when you get started to protect your arms from burns. But this is a matter of choice. Many blacksmiths insist on short sleeves.

- This clothing is not just to protect you from hot iron and steel but to protect you from flying sparks both from the forge and from the hammering you will do.

- Also, wear durable boots. This is because you are going to be dropping hot steel parts. And you need to protect your feet from that. I have seen many people drop hot things out of the forge. Protect your feet!

- When hammering you should wear safety glasses to protect your eyes from flying sparks.

- Ventilation is important – Insure your forge and it's subsequent smoke is adequately ventilated. Do your forging outdoors. If you have a forge indoors or under some kind of structure it has to have a ventilation hood and pipe.

- This one is important – as a beginner you can easily make the mistake of thinking that when the steel is red it is hot! Okay, that's a no-brainer right? But you are also prone to think that when the steel is black it is not hot! And that is not true. Steel can be four hundred degrees and be black. So, while busy and distracted you might want to grab it. Watch out for this mistake. Treat all the metal, including the head of the hammer and the tongs as being dangerously hot.

- As a beginner you should be very cautious when it comes to heating unknown metals. Some can give off a toxic gas. Seek out advice from someone experienced. For now stick with known metals like rebar, railroad spikes, files, truck springs, and purchased metals.

- The best thing you can do in terms of safety is seek out a working blacksmith for advice and help. You can also enroll yourself in a blacksmithing class. They are held all over the country.

Safety Disclaimer

• Blacksmithing is a fun, rewarding and enjoyable pursuit. Yet it is also very dangerous.

• I have made every attempt to point out safety concerns when doing blacksmithing. By its very nature it is extremely dangerous. The fire is so hot that a burn can send you to the emergency room. Please be careful!

And, it isn't just about the fire. The sparks, coals and ash can also burn you very badly. And.... metal gets hot enough to harm you too. Be very careful when doing any kind of blacksmithing.

Remember that even though the heated metal isn't red doesn't mean it isn't dangerous.

• I recommend you only do it under the tutelage of a professional blacksmith.

• One more thing! Never work with galvanized steel. If you heat that steel up it gives off a dangerous toxic fume that can harm you. If you are unsure as to whether your steel is galvanized then don't use it! Or seek out a professional to identify it.

• Thanks and be safe. Always wear the appropriate safety gear including safety goggles.

• Please feel free to email me if you have any safety related questions or concerns. willkalif@comcast.net

What is Blacksmithing?

It is the art and science of shaping steel and iron by first heating it and then manipulating it with a variety of tools.

Blacksmiths use a forge to heat the metals and an anvil and hammer to shape the metals into either a functional form, as in a tool or knife, or into an artistic form such as a sculpture. Or even as a combination of both as in a scroll work wrought iron gate.

So: Heat steel, or Iron, and shape it pretty much sums it up.

This is a very general statement because a smith will use a whole lot of different tools to shape the metals. But the hammer along with the anvil is the most common. We will look at a wide variety of these tools in this book.

Let's take this to a deeper level just to prepare you for more later.

An extremely important aspect of blacksmithing is knowing how steel and iron behaves at different temperatures. It makes sense that the hotter you get the steel the easier it is to work. But you can get it too hot and destroy it. That's one thing. But another just as important thing is that the temperature you heat the steel when working it will have an affect on the steel once it has cooled. This is one of the little known things to beginners.

I can sum it up easily for you.

Take two pieces of the same exact steel. Heat one to a certain temperature and shape it into a knife. Then take the second piece and heat it to a different temperate and shape it into a knife. You end up with two knives that look exactly the same. They use the same steel and have the same shape. But they are significantly different. One will be a great knife that you can sharpen and use. The other will be a terrible knife that will not hold an edge and get dull upon first use or even shatter.

This is the big thing that really makes blacksmithing. How hot, for how long, and when in the process. It is the most important part of the process. And these characteristics change with the type of steel.

And there are hundreds of types of steel. So while it doesn't take a lot to get started in blacksmithing and getting a lot of rewarding work done it is also a craft that can be very in-depth and something you can spend a lifetime learning about.

Part 1 what you need to get started

Note: I have a support web page for all these materials. It includes links and more information about all these supplies and tools: http://www.stormthecastle.com/blacksmithing/blacksmithing-ebook-support-page.htm

Here's the quick list. I will cover all of these one at a time. For now here is what you need.

1. A means of heating steel and iron (some type of forge)
2. Fuel for the forge. Can be either coal or hardwood lump charcoal, or even cord-wood.
3. An apparatus to blow air into the center of the forge (tuyere and blower) Note that tuyere is a fancy name for a pipe.
4. A surface to hammer on (typically an anvil)
5. Some kind of a structure to support your anvil or anvil like object.
6. A metal container for quenching
7. A hammer
8. A pair of tongs or other tool to grip and hold your work
9. A wire brush
10. A screen or grill for the fire-pot
11. Steel you can work with
12. A second steel bucket full of sand so you can cool your hot pieces.

Safety items:

1. Safety glasses
2. Long pants and long sleeve cotton clothes – Cotton because various types of synthetic clothes can actually melt and cause more damage.
3. Durable and strong work boots
4. A fire extinguisher

5. An open-air place to forge for good ventilation

Okay, let's cover these items one at a time.

A Forge

This is the biggest obstacle for you. Let's address this first – And you have plenty of options.

First option: Buying a Forge

Will's quick advice: Well, you have to make a decision here based on what you want to do. Do you think blacksmithing is going to be a big thing for you or possible even a career? Then you definitely should go all in and get yourself a shop forge with a hood and ventilation. I am also going to show you how to make a quick and easy forge. So, read through all of this stuff about forges before you make a decision.

Are you concerned about getting coal or hardwood lump charcoal? Would you like to use plain old cord-wood? That's the kind of wood that people burn in their fireplace. Then you do have the option of buying a Whitlox Forge. They are very reasonably priced and come in various sizes. Check out their website here: whitloxhomestead.com You can get a mini forge for under two hundred dollars and a full size forge for a little over four hundred dollars. (Check their website for current prices) A Whitlox forge is specially designed to get wood burning at higher temperatures.

If you want to use coal in your forge you can get something called a shop forge. This is a good sized all purpose forge that is stationary. You place it somewhere and leave it there. It can burn coal or hardwood lump charcoal. But typically if you are going to purchase a forge like this you should use coal in it.

If you want something smaller you can get a rivet forge. These are typically round in shape and can be moved when needed. You can store a rivet forge somewhere and take it outside when you are going to use it. It can burn coal or hardwood lump charcoal. Typically you stick with coal in a forge like this.

A company with a good selection of shop and rivet forges is CentaurForge.com You also have the option of checking craigslist and ebay.

Another option is for you to get a propane forge. This is a small forge that uses propane tanks as a source of fuel. This is a good option for you if space is at a premium and in particular you are going to focus on making small items, particularly knives.

Blacksmithing with a propane forge can be efficient and effective but I don't recommend you start with it. But, if it appeals to you then you should do a bit more research on it.

Here is a summary of where to look if you decide to buy a forge:

ebay.com (used and new forges)
craigslist.org (used forges)
CentaurForge.com (coal forges)
whitloxhomestead.com (wood forges)
Amazon.com (wood and gas forges)
Atlasknife.com (Good gas forges)|

I have direct links on my website that will help you locate a forge

(http://www.stormthecastle.com/blacksmithing/blacksmithing-ebook-support-page.htm)

Second Option: Make a Forge

Before we make a forge let's get an understanding of what a forge actually is.

A forge is a heat resistant container that holds a fuel while it burns (typically coal). And it also supplies a brisk airflow through a pipe (a tuyere). This airflow flows into the coal causing it to burn hotter than normal.

That's pretty much it. Hold coal, and blow air on it so the coal burns hotter than normal. Everything after that is just details. But let's cover the details too.

We really need these higher temperatures. Wood burns at around 500 degrees Fahrenheit, and it can get up to about 900 degrees. But steel isn't workable until around 1400 degrees. And if we want to weld two pieces of steel together we need the temperature to be around two thousand degrees.

Explanation with diagrams of a forge

So now let's dig deeper and take a look at a basic diagram showing a forge with some things added to it.

Here is a basic forge layout. The fire-pot is where we place the coal or other fuel. The hair dryer or blower forces air through the pipe and up into the fire pot. This forced air causes the fuel to burn hotter.

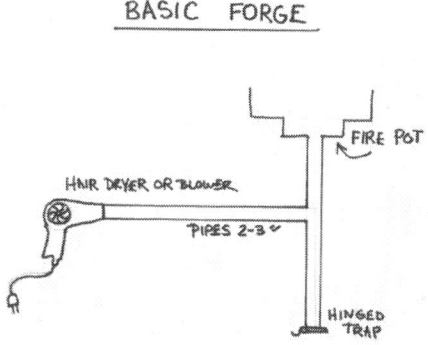

And notice how the pipe also extends straight down from the fire pot. This allows expended fuel, scraps and clinkers to fall out and not clog the fire. It is a trap similar to the trap on a sink. It is important that if you make a forge like this you put a hinge on the bottom of that pipe and that the normal position of the trap is closed. This is so air from the blower doesn't escape that way. You want the air from the blower to go up and into the fire pot.

Not shown in this picture would be an optional venting hood that goes over the fire pot. It would safely vent fumes away. This would be necessary if your forge were indoors or under some kind of roof structure.

Can you see how simple a setup this really is? There are only a couple more things to consider:

The Fire Pot – It is important. The temperature in this area can get extremely hot so you need to make it heat resistant or use something that is very heat resistant. You can use a brake drum from a truck or car to do this. I have done it.

The picture here shows a brake drum from a pickup truck. There is no need to get a new one. A used one is quite adequate. Call or visit a local junkyard and see what they have. You also can try calling local auto repair shops. They will often give you a used one for free or near free. You can see how this makes a nice fire pot. A brake drum is suitable and doesn't itself need any more heat protection. But some kind of other metal structure around the fire pot might need some additional heat protection. You can use refractory cement for this. I will show you pictures of this.

Think of it as using a small metal bathroom sink as your forge. It probably wouldn't tolerate the high heat of forging so you would line the inside of it with refractory cement.

Refractory cement is easy to apply. It is very similar to regular cement and you can buy it premixed and ready to go. It is available on Amazon and is almost always available at your local home improvement store like Lowe's and Home Depot.

Different ways to make a forge

This next picture shows a forge I made. The large green part is where all the coal goes. In the center of it, underneath is where I mounted the drum brake. I welded it in. You could bolt it in if you cannot weld.

That green part for the coal is actually the deck of a lawn mower flipped upside down. It acts as a nice roomy container to hold the coal. And it is tolerant of heat so I didn't need to add refractory cement.

Here is another picture that shows the heart of the system. Here we see the Firepot, the tuyere, and on the end of the tuyere is a rubber hose that I use to clamp on the hair dryer.

At the bottom of the tuyere is a flap. This is the forge. Everything else is just to hold it all together or to hold the coal around the firepot.

It isn't complicated but let's take a look at some final details. You need a way to hold all the pieces together. And you want that firepot to be around hip height. Don't build it at waist height. That is a little too high. It will be uncomfortable to work with.

Building a structure to hold it all.

You can use regular red bricks or cinder blocks to build the major structure that holds the fire pot. Just be sure to line the firepot and around the fire pot with a fire resistant material such as refractory cement or fire bricks.

It isn't complicated but let's take a look at some final details.

Quick and easy structures – Some good ideas on how you can do it.

You can use metal like the lawnmower deck forge I made. I used the handles from the lawnmower as the legs for the forge. And the green piping is from an old swing set.

This setup uses a brake drum and cinder blocks.

Here is another forge that uses cinder blocks.

Another option for you is to cut a steel drum in half longitudinally. I did this to make a forge large enough for sword forging. And I lined it with fire bricks. The tuyere runs the entire length of the inside.

Down and Dirty!!

And here is a very basic setup that doesn't even use a support structure. This system is quick and easy. You can dig a hole and use a metal structure from a grill as the firepot. Just insure you get the tuyere under it. And line the inside with refractory cement so it will last -if needed.

And you can do something like this without a metal container. Dig a hole and line it with fire bricks or refractory cement. If you use firebricks you can then easily dismantle it when you need to.

Let's Review how to build a forge

• Never use any galvanized steel for any part of your forge. It can give off a toxic gas when heated.

• The firepot is the most important thing. It needs to be very heat tolerant. Use a brake drum if you can. If you can't get a brake drum you can use refractory cement and/or fire bricks. Or something that has a thick gauge steel construction.

• Make it sturdy and safe. You do not want it to fall over when you are working hot steel. Secure it well.

• If you build it up you should put the firepot at about hip height.

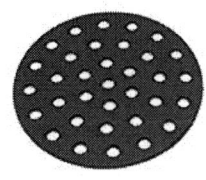

If you build your own forge I recommend you make some kind of a grill to put in the firepot right over the tuyere hole in the middle. This will prevent coal and hot coal from falling down into the tuyere. If you can't make something like this you can use ¼ inch screen. Cut a piece of screen and place it over the firepot hole.

The grill goes right over that hole in the firepot.

Fuel for your forge

There used to be a time when it was challenging to get coal. This has changed. Now you can easily buy it in small quantities on ebay or amazon. I have bought coal many times from amazon.

What type of coal should you get?

For blacksmiths there are three basic types: Bituminous, Anthracite and Coke

Bituminous is a softer coal that doesn't burn as hot. I recommend this type for beginners. It is easier to get going and easier to work with. And as far as the hot goes it is more than hot enough for anything you would want to do.

Anthracite is a harder coal that burns hotter and longer.

Coke burns cleaner and even hotter but is more difficult to light and keep lit. It also requires more airflow. I don't recommend it for beginners.

The picture shown here is of a 25 pound box of bituminous coal that I purchased on amazon. This will get you through half a dozen or more forging sessions. Quite a few total hours of forging. Or course this estimate varies according to how you forge, what you are forging and how big your forge is.

Here is a solid recommendation for you: As a beginner you should stick with Bituminous coal. Once you start to develop some experience you can mix it up in a forging session by starting with bituminous coal and forge a half hour or an hour then mix in some anthracite. This will give you a hotter forge. Don't consider coke for now. That can come to you later.

Option for you to use rather than coal

You can use something called Hardwood Lump Charcoal. It is a hardwood that has been pre-burned under pressure. This causes it to burn hotter than normal hardwood. The thing about hardwood lump charcoal is it's easy availability. You can buy it at any place that sells grilling supplies including home improvement stores.

It typically comes in twenty pound bags.

This is a very convenient option and you will get a couple of sessions out of a single bag. But, the longevity of this is quite different than coal. Twenty pounds of coal will last you a lot longer than twenty pounds of this. Just something to think about.

But the convenience of running down to the Home depot for this is very nice.

Tuyere and Blower for your Forge

The tuyere is the pipe that delivers airflow from the blower and into the firepot. You can use any kind of steel pipe for this. Just not anything that is galvanized. I have used 2" diameter steel plumbing pipe purchased at Home depot and I have used the pipe from an old swing set. Buy or improvise something.

For the blower you can use a hair dryer. With or without a heat setting – it doesn't matter. But if you use it without the heat setting the hair dryer will last longer. You can also get an inexpensive blower just about anywhere including home depot or amazon. Refer to my webpage on supplies for direct links to a blower.

For my sword forge shown in the picture above I have clamped on a heavy duty blower. The clamp was temporary. I later bolted it on.

If you purchase a blower get one with a variable airflow so you have more control over your fire. And just as a reminder be sure it is suitable for house electricity. It will typically be rated for 115 VAC.

Okay, let's talk about anvils

They are a big talking point and people have lots of questions about them. I don't have particularly strong feelings about fancy anvils when it comes to beginners. If you are able to spend several hundred dollars on an anvil then great! Get one. As long as you think you are going to be spending time blacksmithing. A good quality anvil will be instrumental as your skills develop.

But, if you have never done any blacksmithing you don't need anything fancy to get yourself started. Harbour Freight sells a 55 pound anvil pretty cheap. I do recommend you get something that is at least 50 pounds in weight. There are a lot of hobby anvils out there in the 10-20 pound range. These are for hobbies other than blacksmithing – things like silversmithing or jewelry making.

Craigslist is also an excellent place to find used anvils.

 **A used anvil like this one I bought is quite acceptable. Being a rusty color or having some rust on it is ok. You can clean that up and just by using it on a regular basis will shake off a lot of that rust.**

The base of the anvil: This is the thing that the anvil stands on.

Try to get a cut tree stump. That's your best option. But you can make a stand by stacking together 2x4's, 2x6's or 2x8's. Screw them all together tightly and wrap banding around them. The height is important. Build this so the top surface of your anvil is about as high as your mid thigh.

Other tools and materials

Get yourself a two or three pound blacksmith hammer with a cross pein. That's a good place to start. Later on you will develop your own choices and actually end up with a whole lot of specialized hammers.

Here are four of my hammers. The two on the left are cross pien. That refers to the tapered end of the hammer head.

Tongs - This is a tricky subject. You really should get yourself at least one pair of general purpose tongs. You are handling hot steel and you want a good grip on it both for working and for safety. I recommend Wolf Jaw style tongs. This gives you a variety of gripping options. But, if you can't get the tongs use some kind of long handled pliers or vise grips. The longer the handle the better. I have a recommend pair on my website resource page.

A Quench – This is a container to hold water or oil so you can quench or cool off your work. I have used a plastic bucket for this but I recommend you use a steel mop bucket for now. That will keep you going cheaply. At some point in the future when you are forging larger thing you can build or buy a larger quench

A sand bucket – I recommend you fill a metal bucket with sand. You will place hot pieces of metal in it to either cool them or to store them safely while working on other pieces.

A wire brush This is important. As you heat steel and iron a flaky crust will form on it (It is called Scale). You need to brush that off on a frequent basis. Don't start blacksmithing until you get a wire brush.

Setting up your forge

Setting up your forge can be simple and it will vary based on your likes and your height. But generally consider it as a work triangle.

Notice my forge set up here in this picture. I stand at the X. The forge is in the lower left of the picture.

So, where I stand makes it very easy for me to transfer work from forge to anvil without stepping and with minimum twisting of my hips and waist.

That shows the work triangle. The three points of the triangle being the forge, the anvil, and you.

And remember that you can always move things around as you see fit and feel comfortable. And you should adjust the heights of the forge and the anvil so you can comfortably work with little strain on your arms, wrists, elbows, shoulders and back.

Be alert to how your body feels after forging for a period of time. Is your body giving you feedback that something should be changed, moved or modified in height?

PART II – Doing some forging

What steel should you start with?

I have some recommendations for you as a beginner:

✔ You can buy cheap pieces of rebar at any home improvement store. This is a great way to get started and it is readily available. It is sold in the section of the store where they sell bags of cement. This is because rebar is commonly used for cement walls.

✔ You can get railroad spikes. These are terrific to work with – They are soft steel, easy to work and have a good amount of mass to them. (On my resource page I have links to buying railroad spikes online)

✔ You can use woodworking files. These are hardened steel and will need more heat and more work but they are readily available.

Lighting the Forge

Just as a beginner and particularly for the first time you can use lighter fluid to get your forge going. The type that is used to start barbecues.

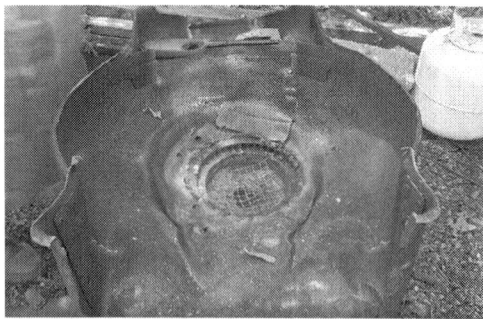

Your forge is nice and clean and you have some kind of grill or screen over the tuyere.

Pour in a generous amount of coal or hardwood lump charcoal. Don't yet turn on the blower. And notice in the next picture how there is some in the center of the forge and there is also quite a lot on one edge of the forge. This is good. Do this. That coal along the edge is for later. You can easily sweep some coal into the center as it is needed.

Now add some charcoal starter and let it soak in according to the directions that come with it.

Light it and keep an eye on it. It may take ten or fifteen minutes to really get going. Once it gets going you can turn the blower on low.

The whole process may take as long as half an hour if this is the first time. If there is existing coal in there that you had fired up before it will get up to temperature much quicker – ten or fifteen minutes. Don't rush things. I know you are anxious to get to the blacksmithing but let the fire do it's thing at it's own pace.

Now let's take a look at a ready fire. And I am going to show you two pictures. The first is with hardwood lump charcoal and the second is with bituminous coal. The two fires are different but when your fire has this nice glow to it you are ready.

(Hardwood Lump Charcoal)   (Bituminous coal)

Let's start by ruining a piece of steel

Yup! You heard me right. We are going to ruin a piece of steel. This will teach us some good things. You can use a file, a piece of rebar, or a railroad spike for this.

Place your piece of steel in the fire and bury it half way into the fire. By half way I mean half the depth into the coal. - Halfway between the top of the coal pile and the hole of the tuyere. Lay the rebar down so it is comfortable resting with a few inches of the end directly in the fire.

BLACKSMITHING FOR BEGINNERS

The Changing Temperature of Steel

While that is heating let's take a look at what is happening. This is an important thing to understand.

As the rebar or steel piece gets hotter it will change color. It will get red, then it will get orange then yellow then white.

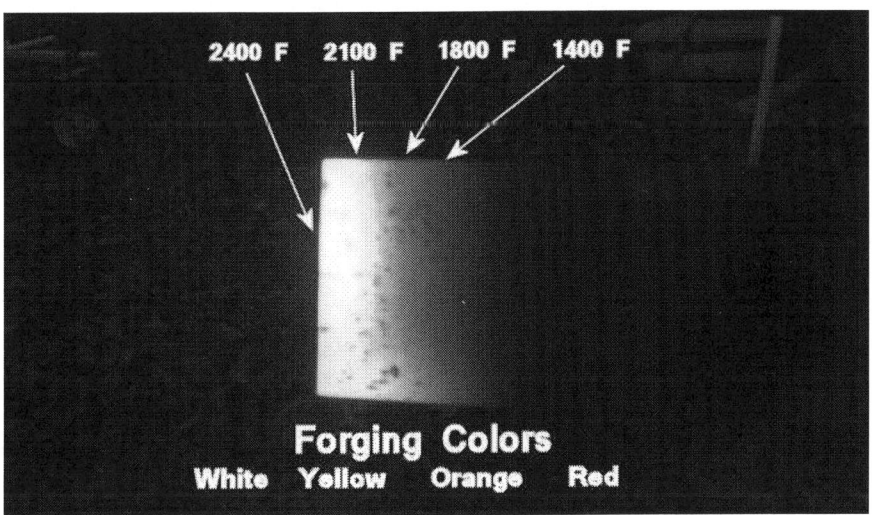

Safety reminder: The far end of the steel is getting hot. And that's easy to see. But the near end where you grab it is black and looks cool. It might not be cool. It could be 500 degrees hot. So, don't grab it with your hand. Grab it with your tongs or pliers.

Feel free to take your piece out and look at it often. This way you can get a feel and a look for how it heats and how long it takes. Notice how it changes through the colors.

This is very important. It is one of the most important skills of the blacksmith. Looking at the steel and knowing where it is at in the heating process.

Keep putting it back in and let it continue to get hotter and hotter.

And notice what happens to it when it gets white hot. It crackles and sparks fly off of it!

That is a bad sign. Remember that cracking and sparking. You don't want that!! It's like miniature fireworks. It's even like a sparkler!

Congratulations! You have done your first blacksmithing and you have ruined your piece of steel! You overheated it. If the piece of steel or iron you are working on gets to white hot and starts sparking you have ruined it!

The end of this rebar or steel is useless to us now. You can cut it off or you can quench it and set it aside. Let's do that. Put it in your water quench and set it in a safe place away from where you are working to let it further cool (preferably in your sand bucket).

Quenching it will not bring it instantly down to ambient temperature. It will still be hot enough to burn you.

Grab another piece of rebar or steel and let's do a little bit more.

The Heat Properties of Steel

You are anxious to make something but take your time. Observe the steel and how it heats. Once the end gets to orange hot you can take it out and give it some hammer blows.

And let's take a look at another property of steel.

It resists heat which is a really good thing. We can use that to our advantage. Notice how the end of the rebar is almost yellow, then there is an orange area then there is a red area. And finally the rest of it is rebar colored.

This is important. It means that the end is much easier to work because it is hotter. So you can go ahead and give it some hammer blows. Try to feel how it reacts both on the orange end and in the red section.

It's very beautiful the way hot steel yields to your hammer blows.

And can see all those black crumbs that fly off the steel? That is something called "Scale". It is impurities being hammered out of the steel. And this is why you need a wire brush for blacksmithing. Feel free to wire brush the rebar anytime it seems to be getting a lot of scale on it.

Let's practice some hammer blows

Go ahead and hammer on it. If the color changes to dark you should reheat it. Repeat the reheat as often as you need. With something like this project there is very little penalty in multiple reheats.

What we are trying to do right now is get some even and flat hammer blows.

You can see this happen if you are getting a nice uniform flatness on the piece. You want the hammer to be parallel to the anvil when it contacts with the steel. This is called Parallel hammering.

This skill is a very big deal. I can't stress this enough. And I recommend you do a lot of this. It will bring your blacksmithing skills up very quickly.

Localized Heating and Cooling

Now let's heat up some of the center section of the rebar. There are a couple of ways we can do this. (And wow! Look at all that scale)

The first way to do this is to place the piece of steel (rebar) in the fire so the desired center section is in the hottest part of the fire. The end of the rebar is sticking through the fire and not getting heated so well.

That technique is easy to understand and very intuitive. You probably could figure that. But there is another way to get specific sections hot. And in the case of this piece the center section.

What you do is heat the end like normal getting a lot of the end and several inches of the rebar orange hot. Then.... You quench just that end an inch or two in water. That will cool the end but not the center section.

This is a very valuable technique and you should practice it. You will use it often. It will allow you to get heat into areas of the piece where you previously couldn't. It's great for doing curves, curls and scrolls. And very valuable when you have worked on the end of a piece and don't want to distort or ruin it with an errant hammer blow.

Why can we do this?

It goes back to what I earlier referred to as steel resisiting heating. The heat doesn't spread well along the length of the steel. It only gets hottest where the forge fire actually is. And this same property of steel also applies to cooling. It will only cool in the specific area where you quench it.

Pointing Steel

Let's do another technique called pointing.

This will teach you more about how to use the hammer. We will use a second hammering technique called angle hammering. And it is just like it sounds. We now want the hammer to impact the steel at an angle.

Angle Hammering

Heat up the other end of your rebar, place it flat on the anvil then hammer it. But this time your hammer is not parallel to the anvil – the hammer is angled.

Continue with this angled hammering and with each strike **rotate the rebar a little bit**. This will form a point! In the case of the picture you see I am holding the rebar in my right hand. This hand is doing the rotating of the bar.

This picture shows you two things. First off you can see we are well on our way to a nice point. But, there is also something else important to notice: I have changed to a lighter hammer! I have switched from a 3 pounder to a 2 pounder. Switching to a new hammer like this enables me to get a finer point. Swinging a lighter hammer is more accurate. And the face of the hammer is smaller which helps too.

Keep that tool switching lesson in mind. You can always try a different tool. And this is why when you visit a blacksmith you will always see dozens of hammers and scores of tongs. Using specific tools can make the job faster and easier – and better with more accuracy.

Now let's take a look at curving and scrolling steel but there is another important concept here. What steps do you need to take and in what order?

Curving Steel

See this rebar knife we are working on?

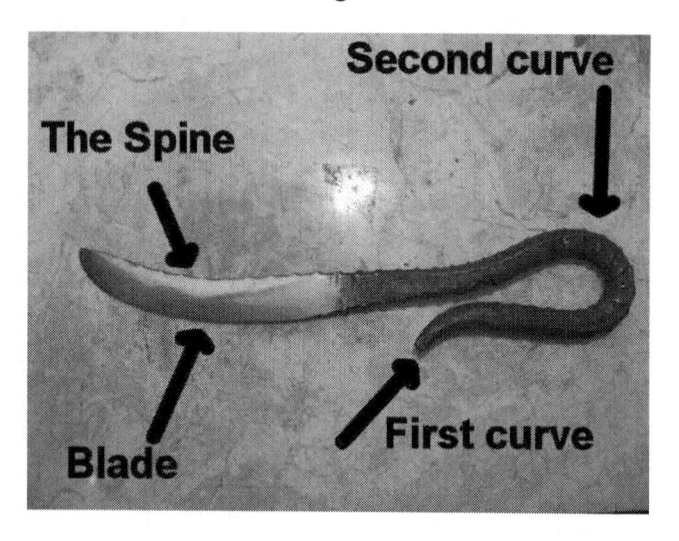

Take a look at the two curves on the right. They are labeled first curve and second curve. When making these curves you would probably be tempted to start by doing the larger curve. But, if you create that curve first it would be near impossible to then create the smaller curve. Simply because you can't get at it with the hammer or other tools.

So we create that curve with some angle hammering. This is the first curve.

And then we can create the second curve. And to do this I used something called a Hardy Tool.

Okay, you can grasp the concept that you sometimes have to work metal in a very distinct series of steps because you wouldn't otherwise be able to get it done.

We can sum it up by saying you should visualize how you want the final product to look like and then break it down into steps so you can achieve it.

I like to do drawings of the process.

And in this part we also looked at two different ways to curve steel. We did it on the anvil with angle hammering and we did it with a hardy tool called a curving tool. There are other ways to curve steel too. You can put one end in a vise and then bend it with pliers or tongs. And you can use the horn of the anvil to do curving.

Using the horn of the anvil is the most common way curving is done. This gives a blacksmith a lot of control over the curve and this is why the horn is shaped in the unusual way it is – like a cone. On the thick part of the cone it is easy to do large curves and on the thinner end of the cone you can do smaller and sharper curves.

The anvil is an amazing thing. Think about it and how to use it. For example when closing this curve into a circle you can place it on the edge of the anvil like this and hammer down on it.

Cutting steel

Another very important technique a blacksmith uses is cutting hot steel. There are many ways to do it and let me show you two.

Using a hot cut off tool and using the edge of the anvil.

You heat your steel to red hot (In the following picture I need to heat the steel more.)

Then you hammer the steel against a sharp edge. You can see that it will cause a notch in the bar.

You can continue to hammer it until the piece is cut, or you can rotate it while hammering. And in the picture you see an "X". You can also hot cut steel on the edge of the anvil.

Want to do some practice?

Try making "S" hooks. These are useful for hanging things on walls, hanging plants and other hooking needs. Try making a variety of them in different sizes, using different techniques and on different parts of the anvil. This will also help you practice hot cutting.

Okay, we have looked at some really useful hammering techniques and other techniques like bending and localized heating. Let's take a closer look at our anvil. I have introduced some things to you that might not be familiar. I will clear that up right now.

Let's take a look at an anvil

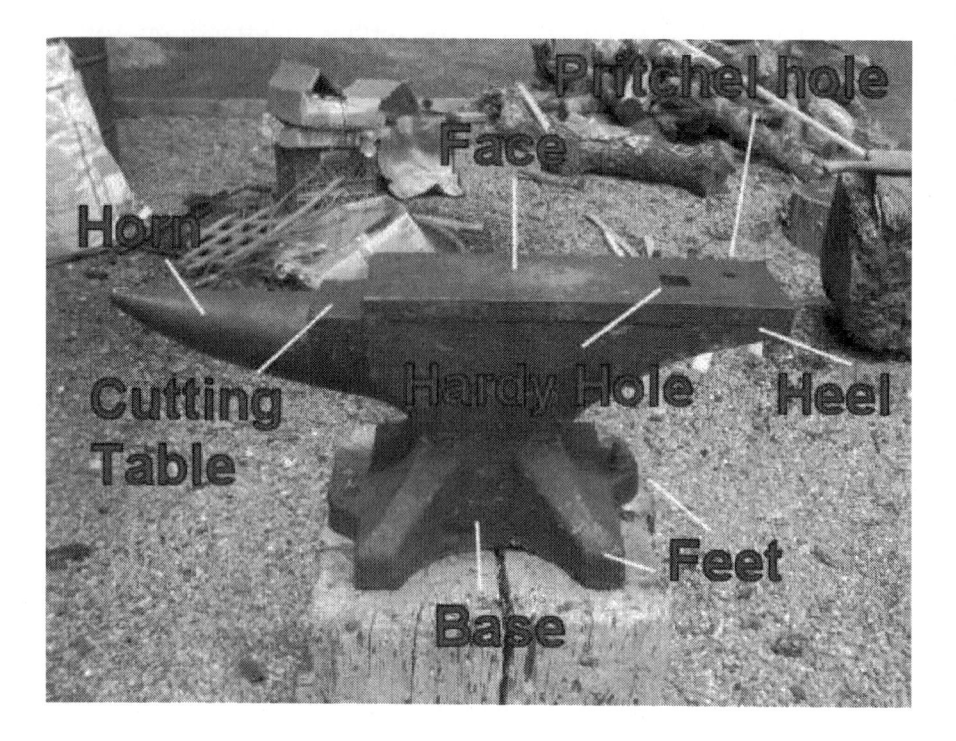

The Horn - We previously looked at the horn and you now understand that it is very useful for curving hot steel. And we also know that the conical shape of the horn means you can use various parts of it to get different size curves. You should have some fun with this and practice different sizes and styles of curves.

The cutting table – This is a little known part of most anvils. This part is specially made to cut hot steel on. You would use this by placing the hot steel on the cutting table then place a chisel down on it and hit the chisel with a hammer.

The Face – Pretty self explanatory. You would do much of your work here on this flat surface. But also note that the edges of the face are also an important tool for working steel.

Now let's take a closer look at those two holes on the face of the anvil.

The Pritchel hole (The round hole) - This is used for punching holes in hot steel. You place a piecd of hot steel over this hole. Then place some kind of piercing tool over it and hit the tool with a hammer. It will pierce a hole in the piece.

The Hardy Hole (The Square hole)

This is a very important and very often used function of an anvil. It is made like this so you can place something called a hardy tool in it. The hole is square so that the hardy tool will not rotate while you are using it.

When bending steel we previously looked at a hardy tool called a curving tool. And in the picture above we see two more tools. The one on the left is a cut off tool for cutting steel and the one on the right is called a swage block it is used to form various shapes.

There are many different shapes of swage blocks.

The effects and importance of Heat

Okay, we have covered a whole lot of blacksmithing stuff in this book and I want to take a look at one more thing -and I alluded to this in the beginning of the book – the effect of different temperatures on steel.

Let's take a look at this chart. It shows how steel changes color at different temperatures.

Fahrenheit	The Color of the Steel
2000°	Bright Yellow
1900°	Dark Yellow
1800°	Orange Yellow
1700°	Orange
1600°	Orange Red
1500°	Bright Red
1400°	Red
1300°	Medium Red
1200°	Dull Red
1100°	Slight Red
1000°	Very Slightly Red, Mostly Grey
800°	Dark Grey
575°	Blue
540°	Dark Purple
520°	Purple
500°	Brown/Purple
480°	Brown
465°	Dark Straw
445°	Light Straw
390°	Faint Straw

The important thing to remember is that you can roughly know the temperature by the color of the steel.

So if you are heating a piece of steel and it gets blue in color what temperature is the steel? It is about 575 degrees! Right!

I recommend you print out this chart and keep it as a handy reference. You might even want to laminate it.

Why is this important?

There are many reasons why you want to know the temperature of steel. First off, and the easy one, is so you can know when to work it.

1500-1800 degrees is the sweet spot for normal shaping and hammering of most steel.

So, when it is bright red to orange-yellow you can work it. And if you have some complex hammering to do and need some extended time hammering it you want to get it up to that 1800 so it stays hot longer – giving you more time to work it.

1900-2000 degrees is the spot where you can do something called "Forge Welding". This is where you actually meld two pieces of steel together. Think of it as welding with a forge. The steel is almost at the point of melting so when hammering the two pieces together they become one piece.

Hardening and tempering steel

This is extremely important when you are blacksmithing tools and bladed objects like knives. And it speaks to the property of the steel after it has cooled.

When you heat steel the molecules in the steel take on a different pattern. And different temperatures create different patterns. If you quickly quench the steel the molecules will stay in this new pattern even after the steel is cooled. And these different patterns have different properties that a blacksmith is looking to achieve.

Let me explain.

If you heat steel to about 1500 degrees (bright red) then quench it in water or oil it will maintain a quality of being extremely hard. That is even once it's cooled completely to room temperature. That's great if you want that property in the steel. But, let's say you are making a knife. Heating it to 1500 and making it very hard means that you can get a very sharp edge on it. It will hold that edge because the steel is very hard. But.... Being hard like that also makes it very brittle. It can easily shatter or snap. And we don't want that in a knife!

So what do knifemakers want?
Well, knifemakers look for some kind of balance called "toughness" we want a certain amount of hardness and we want a certain amount of softness! Yup, that's true.

And they achieve this by heating to different temperatures on different parts of the knife.

Ideally with a knife we want the sharpened edge of the knife to be pretty hard – although not the total hardness we achieved by heating to 1500. And we want the back of the knife (the spine) to be softer. This softness will give the knife a certain amount of flexibility – rather than the knife snapping upon use it will flex a small amount. It will be resilient.

So, how do we do this?

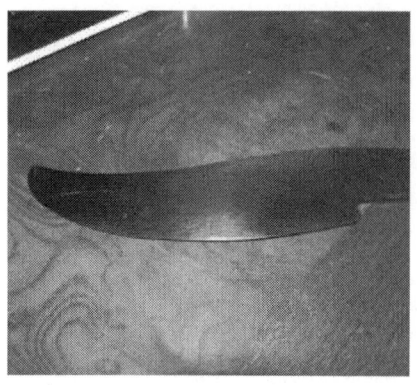

This picture shows you what we have done. I placed the knife near the forge fire with the spine of the knife closest to the fire. What happened is that the spine of the knife heated to a bluish color (575 degrees). This softened it up quite a bit. And the curved bladed section of the knife only heated to a straw color (goldenish). And this heated it less - to about 445 degrees.

What happened is we started with a very hard steel. The whole knife had been heated and quenched at 1500 degrees. The back end was heated to blue which softened it up quite a bit. And the cutting edge was heated to straw color which softened it only a little bit – That edge is still pretty hard.

Now we have a knife that has a slightly softened blade. It will hold a sharp edge but not be brittle.

And the spine of the knife is a lot softer so the knife has some flexibility and toughness.

Now all of this touches into more advanced blacksmithing but it is important for you to know, particularly if you are going to be doing tool making and knife making where the qualities of the finished steel are of the utmost importance.

It is something you can delve deeper into but let's cover one more thing when it comes to heat treatment of steel. That is something called "Annealing".

Annealing

It's an important yet often misunderstood process. But you really should know about it because you are going to run into the term often in your blacksmithing and in particular if you are going to be purchasing steels.

A piece of annealled steel has been softened so that it can be worked on the forge or with power tools and hand tools. That sums it up.

But you can also anneal pieces of steel. And you do this by heating them up to at least 1500 degrees then rather than quenching you allow the piece to cool slowly.

If you were to quench the piece it would be locked into a very hardened state. But if you let it cool slowly the steel will relax into a softer state.

And by slow I mean slow! This depends on the heat and the steel but sometimes you can just let it air cool slowly and that will work. More often you should completely bury the piece in sand so it will cool slower. And a better option would be to bury it in a product called vermiculite. Vermiculite is very resistant to heat. It doesn't want to absorb the heat from your piece so it will take much longer to cool.

And when annealing it is often a good idea to do this whole process of heating then slow cooling at least twice. Some smiths do it three times as a standard.

Where to get steel for your blacksmithing

This is a perpetual challenge for blacksmiths and I can offer you some advice. I touched on this a bit earlier in the book but let me expand on it some more.

The fastest and easiest source is to pick up pieces of rebar at your local home improvement store. You can practice a lot of techniques with it. But it is a very soft steel so you will be limited when it comes to techniques of heat treatment.

You can also try various resources for railroad spikes. This includes purchasing online and going to fleamarkets and swap meets. These spikes are often used by blacksmiths. They have more meat to them than rebar and often times are pretty good low grade mild steel.

Do a search to see if there is an automobile junkyard near you. This is a spectacular place to get lots of good quality steel that you can work with. They will often have bins and racks full of interesting parts you can use in the forge. And among these coveted items are springs and leaf springs from vehicles.

And you can usually request them to be removed from vehicles. I have done this. Gone to a junkyard asking for leafsprings from a small truck. They tell me they will remove them for me and to come back in a couple of days.

So, keep your eyes open. Opportunities will come up and before you realize it you will have a nice collection of materials for the forge.

Lower grade and used steels and irons are ok for general purpose projects that don't need any tempering or heat treatment but if you want to make bladed objects or tools I recommend you start with a known steel. This is for a couple of reasons. First off you know exactly what you have and secondly you will know exactly how to heat treat it.

Different steels react differently to heat treatment. They have different temperatures you have to achieve and some have to be heat treated for specific lengths of time. If you have an unknown steel you really cannot reliably determine how to approach this.

But if you purchase an exact steel you can easily look up it's characteristics and how to heat, forge, work, and heat treat it.

If you are specifically looking to make knives or swords I have a page on my website that explains more about these steels and I include links to purchase them. Right here:

StormTheCastle.com/blacksmithing/selecting-steel-for-knife-making.htm

Okay!

This book is an introductory book. And you are off to a great start. You now have an understanding of many of the basic concepts, techniques, and ideas that blacksmithing employs.

You can go a lot further with your studies and I have a lot of tutorials for you both as written tutorials and video tutorials. I list more on the resources and links page.

One final suggestion

The absolute best thing you can do is seek out a blacksmithing class. They have become very popular and are all over the country. Do a google search in your town or city, or even county for a blacksmith or a blacksmithing course. A variety of different organizations host these classes including Historical Societies, Blacksmithing organizations, technical schools, trade schools and even colleges.

I suggest that you can also cold call a local blacksmith to ask a few questions. Blacksmithis almost always are very willing to share some knowledge and information. This can be very valuable. A local blacksmith will most likely know where you can take courses, what blacksmith you can visit, or where you can get tools, supplies, and even coal.

Thanks for buying my book. Along with this book you get email support from me.

Please feel free to send me an email if you have blacksmithing questions!

My email is: willkalif@comcast.net

Resources, links, and more

Okay, This book is an introductory book. And you are off to a great start. You now have an understanding of many of the basic concepts, techniques, and ideas that blacksmithing employs.

You can go a lot further with your studies and I have a lot of tutorials for you both as written tutorials and video tutorials. Here is a selection of some you might be interested in.

I created a support webpage specifically as a companion to this book. It has resources and links to the many specific tools and products I talk about in this book.

http://www.stormthecastle.com/blacksmithing/blacksmithing-ebook-support-page.htm

The blacksmithing section of my website has hundreds of tutorials that cover just about every conceivable aspect of blacksmithing including knife making, sword making and lots of other projects you can make:

http://www.stormthecastle.com/blacksmithing/index.htm

My youtube blacksmithing videos – I currently have a youtube playlist with 61 blacksmithing videos that cover many aspects of the craft. And I add videos to this playlist on a regular basis. You can find that complete list here: youtube.com/user/epicfantasy

Made in the USA
Middletown, DE
22 September 2022